JUN 1 7 2016

D0943814

Combine a ramp with wheels and axles, and your work becomes even easier!

To start the piano off the truck, we exert a force. A force is a push or pull. We could use our arms to lift the piano, but it's awfully heavy. And lifting would require lots of effort. It makes more sense to roll the piano down the ramp. Careful, Barney!

Aye, aye, Fred!

A ramp makes work easier. Ramps are a type of inclined plane.

Look out below! Stairs and ladders are examples of inclined planes. So is a playground slide. Inclined planes are tools for moving objects from low places to high places. They also help us move things from high places to low places.

Playground slides and water slides are really fun inclined planes!

That's because you used a lot of effort to climb this mountain. The Fred Flintstone way is to use a simple machine! Walking back and forth in a zigzag pattern is like making ramps. Ramps make a climb much less steep. But you have to walk a longer distance.

Fire escapes, ladders, and stairs are all examples of inclined planes.

Simsbury Public Library
Children's Room

Inclined planes help people travel from low places to high places every day.

A ski jump is an inclined plane that creates lots of excitement!

Slopes can have a steep inclination too. The steeper the slope, the faster an object will move down it. And the quicker it will reach the bottom. Look out folks! Here comes Fred Flintstone. I'm going for a gold medal!

Yabba-dabba-doo!

Glossary

exert—to use force to do work

force—a push or pull exerted upon an object

gravity—a force that pulls objects together

incline—to lean or to slope

plane—a flat surface

slope—a slanted surface; one end is higher than the other end on a slope

zigzag—a line or course that moves in short, sharp turns or angles from one side to the other

Read More

LaMachia, Dawn. *Inclined Planes at Work.* Zoom in on Simple Machines. New York: Enslow Publishing, 2016.

Oxlade, Chris. *Making Machines with Ramps and Wedges.* Simple Machine Projects. Chicago: Capstone Raintree, 2015.

Weakland, Mark. *Smash!: Wile E. Coyote Experiments with Simple Machines.* Wile E. Coyote, Physical Science Genius. North Mankato, Minn.: Capstone Press, 2014.

Internet Sites

FactHound offers a safe, fun way to find Internet sites related to this book. All of the sites on FactHound have been researched by our staff.

Here's all you do:

Visit *www.facthound.com*

Type in this code: 9781491484760

Super-cool stuff! Check out projects, games and lots more at
www.capstonekids.com

J
921.8
WEA
$25.00

Index

Look for all the books in the series:

Thanks to our adviser for his expertise, research, and advice:
Paul Ohmann, PhD, Associate Professor of Physics
University of St. Thomas, St. Paul, Minnesota

Published in 2016 by Capstone Press, A Capstone Imprint
1710 Roe Crest Drive, North Mankato, Minnesota 56003
www.mycapstone.com

Copyright © 2016 Hanna-Barbera.
FLINTSTONES and all related characters and elements are
trademarks of and © Hanna-Barbera.
WB SHIELD: ™ & © Warner Bros. Entertainment Inc.
(s16) CAPS35037

All rights reserved. No part of this publication may be
reproduced in whole or in part, or stored in a retrieval
system, or transmitted in any form or by any means,
electronic, mechanical, photocopying, recording, or
otherwise, without written permission of the publisher.

Library of Congress Cataloging-in-Publication Data
Weakland, Mark, author.
  Fred Flintstone's adventures with inclined planes : a rampin'
good time / by Mark Weakland ; illustrated by Alan Brown.
  pages cm — (Flintstones explain simple machines)
Summary: "Popular cartoon character Fred Flintstone
explains how inclined planes work and how he uses simple
machines in his daily life"—Provided by publisher.
Audience: 6–8.
Audience: K to grade 3.
ISBN 978-1-4914-8476-0 (library binding)
ISBN 978-1-4914-8482-1 (eBook PDF)
1. Inclined planes—Juvenile literature. 2 Simple machines—
Juvenile literature. I. Brown, Alan (Graphic designer),
illustrator. II. Title. III. Title: Adventures with inclined planes.
IV. Series: Weakland, Mark. Flintstones explain simple
machines.
TJ147.W393 2016
621.8—dc23   2015024732

Editorial Credits
Editor: Alesha Halvorson
Designer: Ashlee Suker
Creative Director: Nathan Gassman
Media Researcher: Tracy Cummins
Production Specialist: Kathy McColley

The illustrations in this book were created digitally.

Image Credits
Shutterstock: Herbert Kratky, 19, Mark William Richardson,
15, prudkov, 10, RioPatuca, 9; Thinkstock: Brand X Pictures,
5; Wikimedia: Niagara, 17

Printed in the United States of America in
North Mankato, MN. 092015 009221CGS16